Conquering Twitter In 10 Minutes A Day

By Katharine Grubb

Conquering Twitter In 10 Minutes A Day

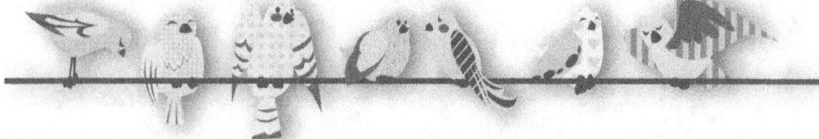

For Sheri, Jessica, Joanna, Ian, Eric, & Aryeh

TWITTER ALWAYS REMINDS ME OF ATTENDING A SOLD-OUT NFL GAME IN A HUGE STADIUM.

When I'm on Twitter, I figuratively stand up and yell and yell as loud as I can, hoping to get someone's attention. Everyone on my right, my left, below me, and above me is doing the same thing. We're yelling about our interests, our passions, our causes or the books we wrote and no one is paying attention. Occasionally, someone may wave at me, but when he does, he's only telling me that I should download the first chapter of his free book, *Amish Zombie Princesses*. I pass. The person in front of me hears me yelling. He turns around and says, "Wanna follow me?" I say, "Sure!" And then he says, "Great! But can you like my Facebook page too?" I brush him off. I yell more, and someone three people over waves at me. I wave back. She says, "This is crazy!" And I say, "It is!" And then I make a joke and she laughs and she makes a joke and I laugh and she follows me and I follow her and then we talk a bit more and I say to myself, *Finally! A friend!* I see her over and over again and we have more conversations. It turns out she's written a book about learning to run in her 40s and I say, "Really?

Me too!" And I buy her book. Later, when my book comes out, she is one of the first people I tell. She buys it, reads it, reviews it, shares it on her blog and connects me with other readers.

This illustration is an exaggeration. Twitter really isn't millions of people yelling at each other in a crowded stadium, but it's similar in a lot of ways. But that last relationship? The one about the woman who bought my book? That's happened to me dozens of times. I have made many, many relationships through Twitter.

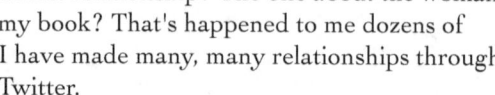

I believe that there are other people out there to engage with, to laugh with, to learn from and eventually to support because I want to. **I also believe that with a thoughtful plan, *anyone* can use Twitter to find the right audience which will, hopefully, build into an enthusiastic tribe who will buy the book, like the page, download the sample, join the group or sign up for the newsletter.** And with a group of raving fans, the figurative crowd and noise of Twitter seems easier to manage.

HOW DO WE ENGAGE OTHERS? HOW DO WE GROW AN INFLUENTIAL PLATFORM ON TWITTER?

I believe you can conquer Twitter with a well-crafted, thoughtful strategy for the long-term, that is built up slowly, maybe even one reader at a time.

This **workbook will show you how to create a long-term Twitter presence. It approaches your Twitter activity in three parts: your set-up, your strategy and your system.** This book is not a guarantee of success. But what it will provide for you, is an orderly, thoughtful process in your brand, your biography, your target market, and your future tweets. The best way to use this book is to work through it at least 10 minutes a day. Throughout the sections, exercises are provided to help you think about yourself, your brand, your books and your goals on Twitter. This isn't a project that needs to be rushed through. It is far better to be thoughtful about your answers than to slap something together because you are in a hurry. This book was originally intended for authors who want to use Twitter to build their tribe of readers, but the principles of it are universal. Anyone with an interest in using Twitter as a marketing tool would find this book useful.

IF YOU DO ALL OF THE EXERCISES IN THIS BOOK, YOU WILL:

-- Build a general blueprint of your brand that you can build on in the future.

-- Write a clear, inviting biography full of engaging, specific nouns.

-- Identify your market so you know where to look for followers.

-- Identify key words that are valued in your target market.

-- Use lists to follow others in your key market.

-- Consistently follow people in your key market on a regular basis.

-- Actively engage with old and new followers.

-- Create interesting and inspiring content that is consistent with your brand.

-- Practice linking to other social media frequently.

-- Retweet and favorite tweets from followers on your lists.

-- Organize your time so that you can meet these requirements with a minimum of energy and fuss.

> ALSO, INCLUDED IN THE WORKBOOK, IN THESE BOXES, ARE A FEW "TWITTER DON'TS!" THESE ARE THE BIG FAUX PAS THAT TURN OFF MORE FOLLOWERS THAN TURN ON. I'VE ALSO INCLUDED "AUTHOR CONFESSIONS," WHICH EXPLAINS SPECIFIC THINGS I'VE DONE WITH TWITTER TO GAIN FOLLOWERS AND BUILD MY TRIBE.

THE BOOK IS DIVIDED IN THREE SECTIONS:

1) **Set-up:** This includes serious thinking about your brand, your purpose, your bio, your key words and your target market. The set-up phase is the single most important part of this book. You can use the information you've collected from this section in any social media strategy. Don't neglect this section. Don't rush through it.

2) **Strategy:** This is what you'll do with all your set up information. In this section, you'll learn how to find followers within your target market, how to schedule tweets, how to create useful lists, and you'll understand what types of tweets are the most interesting and retweet-worthy. All of this will help you to engage

with followers. Engagement is the ultimate goal. You can't have raving fans without engagement.

3) Systems: In this section, I break down your daily, weekly and monthly maintenance lists for Twitter. I separate the must-dos from the optional, so you can pick and choose how you want to spend your daily time on Twitter. Ideally, you can do these in 10 minutes a day, but like every other social media platform, it is easy to get distracted. You can *always* add more time to Twitter and as you develop relationships, you may find that you want to.

TWITTER DON'T: DON'T EXPECT TWITTER TO WORK LIKE FACEBOOK; IT'S A DIFFERENT ANIMAL ALTOGETHER. FACEBOOK IS LIKE HAVING A BIG MEAL AT APPLEBEE'S WITH YOUR BUDDIES FROM HIGH SCHOOL, YOUR COLLEGE ROOMMATES AND YOUR PARENTS. TWITTER IS LIKE GOING TO A SOLD-OUT PROFESSIONAL FOOTBALL GAME IN GILLETTE STADIUM AND HAVING A CONVERSATION WITH THE PEOPLE NEXT TO YOU, WHILE YELLING AT THE GUY ON THE OTHER SIDE CHEERING FOR THE OTHER TEAM.

You must work through these three sections in order. No cheating and jumping ahead. Even if you already have a Twitter account and followers, you can tweak and modify what you've done to make it more effective. The exercises are designed in such a way that you can give this workbook 10 minutes of your time daily and accomplish the goals. Set your timer if you must.

So let's get started! Get a pencil! We're Conquering Twitter in 10 Minutes A Day!

THE SET-UP

In this section of the workbook, you will be fine-tuning general ideas of your brand, writing your Twitter biography, and understanding what it means to have a good photo. The more you consider these things, the more successful you will be in engaging others. Each of the exercises in this section have to do with creating your identity and persona. Take your time. Spend as many 10 minute increments as you need to figure this out for yourself.

WHAT IS BRANDING?

Branding is a combination of what we present to the world and what we really are. Your brand is what people say about you behind your back. Your brand is a combination of feelings and impressions that readers associate with you. Your brand will be visible in your logos and graphic designs, but it's also evident in your tweets and how you present yourself to others. A brand is kind of like a professional reputation. It's kind of a creative identity. A brand includes your books and your genre, but adds in your personality, your appearance and your interactions.

If you are just starting out as a writer, you may not have developed a brand. You may not have created that reputation. Your persona may not yet be known to many. That's okay. Don't be in a rush to define who you are. The exercises in this section are here to guide you in fine-tuning your brand, but it is not the conclusive statement on who you are. It is not out of the ordinary for an author to adjust his branding as his career progresses. You can do that too.

What does it mean to have a brand as a writer? *You're that guy who writes all those mysteries that take place in the North Georgia woods. You're that energetic lady who writes books about cocker spaniels. You're the writer whose fantasy stories are so funny. You're the poet who talks about his cat.* This is only an example. Brands can be even more precise. Think about your favorite authors and how you would describe them in one sentence. If your one sentence is an accurate one, then you are getting close to their brand.

EXERCISE 1.1

This exercise is designed to have you think about the books you've already written and the books you're going to write. Each question is about you, so there is no right or wrong answer. Take 10 minutes a day to think about these questions thoroughly. Don't rush this. Ask others who know you well for input. Then as you make notes, keep your answers in a safe place so you can refer to this later. If you can't answer a question, skip it and move on. Not all of the questions are necessarily applicable.

1. Do you see any repeated themes in your work? What are they?

2. Do you return to the same genres, settings, medium, subject, form? Which ones? Why?

3. What 10 adjectives best describe your work?

4. What mood do most of your pieces convey? Are they light and hopeful? Are they dark?

5. What complimentary things have others said about your work? Make sure these are specific and clear.

6. What is it about your books that set them apart from others?

7. What strengths do you have that are visible in your books? For example, your sense of humor? Your word play? Your passion for social causes?

8. When you have an engaging conversation with people about your books, what is it that you usually talk about?

9. Have you ever been introduced in an unusual or memorable way? What did the introducer say about you?

10. Do you have an unusual method to your books that you're particularly proud of? My method is to write in 10 minute increments, so becoming the 10 minute writer was an easy step. Can you do that with your method?

EXERCISE 1.2

What moods or emotions do you most frequently want your readers to engage in when they read your books? (This is an important question. We'll be returning to it later.) Choose at least three, but no more than seven descriptors that you'd like associated with your brand. Can't find what you want? Write in any adjectives that you need.

Accessible	Amusing	Benevolent	Belligerent
Calm	Carefree	Cautious	Cheerful
Common	Compassionate	Confident	Conforming
Creative	Curious	Defiant	Determined
Disbelieving	Elite	Enthusiastic	Evasive
Excited	Faith-filled	Frugal	Frustrated
Gentle	Gloomy	Graceful	Happy
Helpful	Humble	Hysterical	Indignant
Innocent	Intelligent	Joyful Melancholy	
Mischievous	Optimistic	Practical	Protective
Proud	Provocative	Puzzling	Savvy
Serious	Silly	Streetwise	Stylish
Sure	Thankful	Thoughtful	Timeless
Tranquil	Trendy	Uplifting	Wise
Witty	Zealous		

Note: Just because you want to be known for these positive qualities doesn't mean you will be. You only have so much control over your brand. The true character of you, your work, the way you treat others and your business practices will color your brand far more than any exercise in any book. Be the type of person you want to be known for.

WHAT IS A BIOGRAPHY?

Your biography (we're going to say *bio* to save characters!) is the first impression you make on others. Your bio is your handshake, your business card, your free sample. If you want to be taken seriously, if you want to attract others, if you want to engage with readers, if you want your brand to be known, you need to put care into creating your bio.

Your bio is not your resume'. Save that for LinkedIn. Your bio is not a sales pitch. Your bio is not a list of the books you have written. It is not a chance to show off your awards. It isn't where you mention your agent. Why? *Because none of these facts will attract a reader to you.* Instead, your bio should be a list of nouns that show the real you. *"Poodle lover. Vegan cook. Mom of 7. Crochet enthusiast. Neurosurgeon."* Diverse nouns that describe who you are can be gateways into conversations. Conversations create engagement. Engagement builds relationships. Relationships build tribes. These are precious words. You don't want to waste them.

This section will walk you through the search for the perfect nouns that describe you. Like the last exercises, do not feel like you need to rush through them. Rather, take your time to nail it perfectly.

EXERCISE 2.1

In 10 minutes, brainstorm for as many true and accurate nouns that apply to you. Don't worry about whether or not they fit your brand. Don't worry about counting your characters. Go for specific, not general. This is your first draft and it can be wicked long. In fact, if you can get 25 nouns that describe you, I'll mail you a gold star. (Also? As tempting as it is to be funny, you want to represent yourself honestly to your tribe, so don't say you're an FBI agent, a supermodel or a mad scientist unless you *really* are one.)

Here are a few hints:

1. Nouns about your family situation and be specific! *Mommy, Widower, Adoptive parent*

2. Nouns about what you do during the day: *Homeschooler, Librarian, Lion Tamer, CPA, astronaut*

3. Nouns about what your passions are: *Independent Author, Water color artist, Jazz Bassoonist*

4. Nouns about your hobbies, if you want to talk about them: *Bird watcher, Mystery reader, Cigar enthusiast*

5. Nouns about your personality, but try to come across as humble, not obnoxious: *Joke teller, Punch line predictor, Curmudgeon, Wallflower, Contemplator, Overthinker, Non-conformist.* (Don't call yourself smart, funny, beautiful, hot, or talented, even if it's true.)

6. Nouns that connect you to your target market: *Conservative, Jedi, Fangirl, PTSD survivor*

7. Any other noun that accurately describes you that has the potential for starting a conversation: *fidgeter, popcorn hater, poodle lover, coupon cutter, Patriots fan.*

Note: The nouns that you choose to be in your bio should only be those that you *want* to have conversations about. If you don't want the world to know about your family, your chronic illness, your criminal record, your Taylor Swift obsession, or your cuticle-picking habit, *don't mention it!*

> **AUTHOR CONFESSION:** FOR EXAMPLE, ONE OF MY BOOKS IS CLEAN ROMANCE. IT'S A BOOK THAT PROMOTES CHIVALRY AND CHASTITY. FROM A POLITICAL POINT OF VIEW, I'LL PROBABLY HAVE MORE READERS FROM CONSERVATIVE CIRCLES THAN FROM MORE LIBERAL ONES. I NEED TO KEEP THIS IN MIND.

EXERCISE 2.2

After you've collected your nouns, choose the best ones. Look for the ones that have the most meaning, the ones that show a unique you, the ones that are most likely to spark conversations. The best nouns have meaning: they give the world a picture of the uniqueness of you. Toss out the nouns that are unimportant or that anyone can say, like *coffee drinker, chocolate lover, breather of oxygen.* Arrange them from most general to most specific. Or arrange them in a way that your target market can recognize them. You know how ingredients on a food item are listed from most significant to least? Arrange your nouns the same way.

EXERCISE 2.3

Go back to Exercise 1.2 in the section about branding. In that exercise, you listed emotions that you wanted associated with your brand. Make sure that the nouns you chose in your bio are consistent with those emotions. For example, if you want to be known for being compassionate, then your noun, *poodle lover,* is consistent. But if you want to be known as humble, yet you have nouns like *future Pulitzer Prize winner, hot mama,* or *social media expert,* then you're sending the wrong message. If you want to be known as well-read, don't mention that you binge watch *America's Next Top Model.* Either change your nouns or change the emotional goals of your brand.

EXERCISE 2.4

Add the final touches, but do it with your market in mind. For example, emojis will make your brand look juvenile; only add them if you are targeting a young market. Hashtags can be hard on the eyes, use them sparingly. Give a location, but keep it general; your home state or country, but not your city. Only mention team names if fans are your target market. As much as you love your children, you don't need to tell us their names and ages unless you have a specific marketing reason to mention this. And everyone's children are *amazing.* Mine especially. You don't need to waste characters on empty and self-serving adjectives. Don't mention your pets unless you really want to talk about them or your market includes them. The same can be said for husbands.

EXERCISE 2.5

Add a photo. The best choice is a real photo of you, not your dog, not a cartoon version of you and certainly not the stick drawing from your daughter. A professional headshot is the ideal, but if you can't do that, a nice, non-bathroom selfie will work too. I suggest using the same photo across all your social media platforms and *not changing it.* Your tribe will find you by sight first, and you don't want to confuse them or get lost because you *had* to put your team's logo up for the championship. Also? Your photo has to be consistent with your brand too. Serious literary writers should not have cutesy selfies with duck faces.

Congratulations! You are now ready to set up on Twitter!

The Strategy

This is the section of the workbook that will help you understand your target market, key words to look for, whom to follow, how to schedule, how to create lists, use the lists of others and what kind of content your followers will receive from you. This is a complicated section that will require much thought. Take your time in it. You can give this section 10 minutes a day and still make progress. As I said in the previous section, your ultimate goal is engagement so that your tribe grows. By the time you're done, you'll know exactly what to tweet and who to follow. This section is worth doing well and thoroughly. Let's get started!

Strategic Targeting

You are a writer. That means that you want readers who will not only buy your books, but also become your raving fans who will buy *everything* you write. This never happens in the first conversation anyway. If your strategy up to this point has been, "be my friend, but first buy my book!" then you aren't looking for engagements, and you're certainly not looking for a long-term relationship with a raving fan. But, if your strategy is to look first for others who want conversations, who can receive your generosity, who would be genuinely interested in your work, who will resonate with your art, then your chances are far better for success. **Your *market* is the group of people who are the most likely to fork over dough for your book.** The key phrase is *most likely.*

How do you find them?

On Twitter, you do this through key words, searches, lists, hashtags and chats. Each on of the following exercises will show you what to do.

EXERCISE 3.1

Start with your work. Non-fiction writers have the advantage: if they write cookbooks, they look for readers who like to cook, if they write parenting books, their readers are the same people who buy Pampers. If they write books about writing novels in 10 minute increments, then they know that other writers are interested. But *fiction* writers have a much tougher time with this. The nouns or key words that you mention in your book could be helpful in finding readers.

1. For the next 10 minutes, brainstorm for as many nouns that you can come with that can be associated with your genre or sub-genre. For example, detective mysteries have an unsolved crime and the criminal is discovered by a law enforcement officer. The nouns *crime, mystery, law enforcement, detective,* can all be used as key words for this sub-genre. List as many genre-related words as you can.

2. Then, for 10 minutes, list as many specific nouns that   have to do with your setting (the city, state, country) your story takes place in. For example, my book *Soulless Creatures* takes place in Norman, Oklahoma at The University of Oklahoma. *Norman, OU, and Oklahoma* are all important nouns. I could also add *Bible Belt, Southern Plains, Texas, Oklahoma City, Tulsa.*

3. For 10 more minutes list nouns associated with the specific time and culture of your story. Be as specific as possible. For

example, my book *Soulless Creatures* takes place in the 1986-1987 school year, I can list *80s, 1986, pop music, Ronald Reagan, New Wave,* etc.

From the three lists, try to come up with 25 nouns total. You will use this list later for exercises to find followers. You can also use this key word list for any other need you will have in your marketing.

EXERCISE 3.2

Next? Let's think about people who like to read that genre. This exercise collects nouns and adjectives that can apply to your target market. You are trying to get as broad a picture as possible of your ideal reader. Take as many 10 minute increments as you need an ask yourself these questions about the people who read your genre. If you don't know the answer, do a little research. You can Google "What kinds of people read romance?" and find many clues.

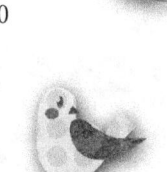

1. How old is your ideal reader? Can you determine a group, like 15-25 years old? Over 45?
2. What gender is your ideal reader? Generally speaking, women read more romance books than men do, and men read more thrillers than women. Do your books fall along gender lines? If they don't, don't worry about it.
3. What is the family life like for your ideal readers? Are they married? Single? If they have children, about how old would they be?

4. What kinds of jobs would you expect your ideal reader to have? Write down occupations that could be common among readers of your genre.

5. What kinds of things do people who enjoy your genre get into? For example, readers of military thrillers may be into sports, NASCAR, biographies, air shows, trucks, hunting, etc. Your ideal reader has hobbies too. What could they be?

6. What kinds of political opinions does your ideal reader have? Readers of Christian fiction are generally more

conservative politically than readers of erotica.

7. What kinds of economic levels do readers of your genre have? For example, readers of literary works are probably in a different socio-economic status than readers of steampunk.

8. What kinds of education does your ideal reader have? Are they high school-educated? College-educated? Advance degree?

9. What kinds of cultural preferences does your reader have? Are they along nationality lines? A specific people group? Do you have a multicultural story? What television shows would they watch? What kinds of products would they buy?

10. Is your ideal reader connected to a geographic location? A specific country? City? Is your ideal reader more urban or rural?

AUTHOR CONFESSIONS: SOMEONE DESCRIBED MY BOOK AS THE "ANTI-50 SHADES OF GREY". THIS WAS A PERFECT COMPARISON. I USED IT TO MARKET FALLING FOR YOUR MADNESS. I HADN'T THOUGHT OF IT.

EXERCISE 3.3

With the information you have just collected, you can create a picture of your ideal reader. Fill in this sentence:

My ideal reader is a _____(man or woman) around _____ years of age. Their family situation probably looks like _____.
They may work in the _____, _____, _____, _____, or _____ fields.
They may have these five interests as hobbies or pastimes: _____, _____, _____, _____, and _____. When they vote, they generally vote _____. They may be considered part of the

_____ socio-economic class. They may educated up through _____. Their culture may mostly be _____. And geographically, I am more likely to find them in _____, _____, or _____.

TWITTER DON'T: THE DM FOLDER IS FOR ALL YOUR PRIVATE MESSAGES. OFTEN PEOPLE ON TWITTER USE IT TO SEND MESSAGES AUTOMATICALLY TO THEIR NEW CONNECTIONS. IT'S KIND OF LIKE BUGGING THEM AGAIN. THE GENERAL CONSENSUS AMONG WRITER TYPES IS THAT IT'S ANNOYING AND SPAMMY. AS TEMPTING AS IT IS TO BROADCAST YOUR AWESOME AT EVERY AVAILABLE OPPORTUNITY — - LET PEOPLE USE THEIR DM FOLDER FOR IMPORTANT THINGS AND SINCERE DIRECT COMMUNICATION.

EXERCISE 3.4

Make a list of 50 to 100 nouns or adjectives that you can associate with the sentence you filled in Exercise 3.3. For example, if your ideal reader is a stay-at-home mother of toddlers, then important nouns to her would be *diapers, day care, preschool, kindergarten, toys,* etc. Go back through all your exercises and collect them. These are your key words. You are going to use these later for searches to find followers. These key words have value to your target market, so they should have value to you.

Strategic Following

Every social media platform has its subculture and Twitter is no different. On Twitter, the general way to find followers is to follow someone first. This practice doesn't translate well to Facebook or Pinterest, but on Twitter, this is the way it's done. If you want to be found, you have to seek others first. Sadly, just because you have a great bio and can write a clever tweet or two, it doesn't mean the world will flock to you. You have to go find the world   and get its attention. In this section, the exercises will explain to you how to find followers using the key words from the last section. Once you find people to follow, you can choose to follow them instantly, or you can carefully analyze their Twitter activity to see if you have a good fit for your target market. There are advantages and disadvantages to both methods. This section will show you how to do each. Ideally, you should follow 50-100 people a day but the more time you spend over every bio, the more time this will take. Start with 10 minutes per day, and then, as your followers increase or as you grow in your skills, add more time to this project.

EXERCISE 4.1

Return to your notes from Exercise 3.4 and do a search on Twitter for each of those nouns, for example, *diapers*. The search will reveal every time someone has mentioned *diapers* in a tweet. Who tweets about diapers? Moms of infants and toddlers. If those people are your target market, you should follow them. This method translates well to any target market if you think about the types of nouns that are important to them. Take 10 minutes and go down the list of nouns from 3.4, using them as searches. Then follow as many people as you can. Stop when your 10 minutes is up or you've followed 25 people. Because you collected so many nouns and key words, you will never lack for a starting point. This exercise will be mentioned again in the section called Systems and you can use it repeatedly as you grow your followers.

TWITTER DON'T: Don't ever sign up for TrueTwit Validation. This is the polar opposite of the DM. It's standoffish and aloof. If you're on social media and you have an intention to engage with others yet you make them jump through a hoop to meet you, then you're not being very nice. It's like shaking hands at a party but making everyone wear rubber gloves because you're afraid of germs. It's like kissing with a protective tissue on your mouth. NO. Don't do it. If you can't stand the possibility of spam, then the internet is not for you.

WHILE KEY WORDS ARE A GREAT TOOL TO FIND FOLLOWERS, THEY AREN'T THE ONLY WAY. LISTS ARE ALSO A GOLD MINE FOR POTENTIAL READERS.

EXERCISE 4.2

If you have begun to follow people, some will follow you back. Don't ignore them. Say hi! Read their bio and ask a question: *I love dogs too! What do you have?* Or, *Pennsylvania! Where? I lived in Pittsburgh!* Even though these type of conversations are often just small talk and superficial, they are the foundations of a relationship. Your tribe's growth has to start somewhere, so start with simple conversations. Remember though, this is *not* the time for a sales pitch or a request to like your page. That comes later and it's worth waiting for.

EXERCISE 4.3

Many people on Twitter have done your work for you. They've organized their followers into lists and if they've made the list public, you can see exactly who is on it. You can also follow everyone on others' lists! Set your timer for 10 minutes. Choose one follower on the Twitter website and look at lists. You'll see two options: *subscriber* and *member*. Click member and you'll see all the lists that other people have put this person. To further explain this: I know that I want to target writers. I find a well-known author's name on Twitter, say, Stephen King. I look at what lists he's on. Someone has put him on a *Cool Writers* list. I go through the list and follow everyone that would potentially fit my target market. (I don't follow Stephen King because he'll probably never buy my book.) You can do the same thing. This works best if you are specific about the target market that you are looking for.

EXERCISE 4.4 (Optional)

This exercise explains how you can analyze someone's Twitter information to find whether or not they are a good fit. This method takes time; 10 minutes may not yield many followers. But because of the extra analysis, it has the potential of being worth the effort.

1. Look at the photo: Is their photo consistent with someone in your target market? Let's say you write Amish fiction for the Christian market. It's a good guess that a bikini-clad 19-year-old would not be a potential reader. Don't follow them.

2. Look at their numbers. Each Twitter bio has three numbers: how many tweets this person has posted, how many followers he has, and how many people follow him. This is good information. Your ideal follower is someone who is on Twitter frequently, so if he has less than 500 tweets, he may not be worth the trouble. Also, if there is a gap between his follower/follow numbers of bigger than 20%, then it could be that he isn't interested in interaction. You are looking for followers who are more likely to follow you back and engage. If that's not a possibility, don't bother.

AUTHOR CONFESSION: I DO NOT FOLLOW PEOPLE WHOSE PHOTOS ARE THE GENERIC EGG ICON, WHO ARE NOT FULLY DRESSED NOR HAVE PROVOCATIVE IMAGES IN THEIR BIO. I'M LOOKING FOR THE PEOPLE WHO ARE MOST LIKELY TO BUY MY BOOK, NOT WEIRD EXCEPTIONS TO THE RULE.

CONVERSATIONS ‹ ENGAGEMENTS ‹ FRIENDSHIP ‹ RAVING FANS ‹ LIFETIME OF SALES

3. Look at their feed: Scroll down and read their last 10-20 tweets. Good candidates have a variety of things, like RTs, conversations, links, images. Good candidates have conversations with others, are generous and interesting. Not-so-good candidates have only things like "buy my book" tweets, quotes, links to their blogs, "like my Facebook page!" and other self-promotion tweets that seem to go only one way. You can always unfollow someone if they get annoying.

Strategic Engagement

NOW THAT YOU KNOW HOW TO FOLLOW PEOPLE IN YOUR TARGET MARKET (AND HOPEFULLY THEY'RE FOLLOWING YOU BACK,) YOU NEED A PLAN TO ENGAGE WITH THEM GENEROUSLY. THIS IS WHERE THE WORK COMES IN.

You should not create your followers without something to give them. Business guru Scott Aughtmon wrote an infographic, *21 Types of Content We All Crave.* This graphic explains how certain types of material is attractive to readers and none of it is general information or sales. (Do a search for this graphic on Pinterest and save it! It is worth having!) Instead, crave-worthy content speaks to the heart of the reader, it encourages, it gives instruction, it narrates, it inspires, it explains, it directs and it comforts. If your purpose is to build genuine relationships, then you must speak to the heart of your followers. And this *is* possible in 140 characters.

Your default strategy on Twitter should be generosity. All of your tweets should be, in the beginning, based in giving, not taking. A generous message is one that reveals truth to someone else. A generous message is one that engages someone else. A generous message is one that opens a doorway. A generous message is one that says, "hey, let's do this together!" A generous message is one that champions the weak and needy. A generous message is one that recognizes strengths in others. A generous message is one that dwells on the positive. A generous message is one that is looking to connect with others, not looking for sales. A generous message is one that is infectious, will draw others in, establishes the messenger as a friend and can grow lifelong relationships.

How do you know if you are generous? You're not if you're obsessed with only numbers. You're not if you're reading this thinking, "when do we get to the part where I gain 20,000 followers?" Or, "when do I get to tell the world about my book?" You're not if you're on Twitter because someone told you you should be. You're not if you aren't interested in the struggle and stories of the people around you. How do you do this, when all you are trying to do is build your writer's platform?

You return to your brand. You go back to what you want to be known for and formulate a way to give generously to followers.

The following exercises are designed to help you envision how you will be generous to others on Twitter. They also explain ways that you can combine crave-worthy content with your brand. They explain how to use hashtags to start conversations, tweet your blog well and start a chat. Exercises 5.1 and 5.2 are important and should be prioritized. The other exercises are optional.

EXERCISE 5.1

Return to Exercise 1.2 and review all of those emotions that you want tied to your brand. Then check off the following items, based on Aughtmon's 21 Types, that would be consistent with the moods and emotions you want to be known for. You will not be able to check off all of these, but you will be able to check several. Aim for six that you would find to be the easiest to do.

1. I can remind my readers that life is beautiful and meaningful.

2. I can remind my readers that dreams come true.

3. I can remind my readers of the big picture.

4. I can remind my readers that they are valuable.

5. I can remind my readers of foundational truths and concepts.

6. I can surprise my reader.

7. I can tell my reader stories. (This is different from *sell* my reader stories.)

8. I can take my reader on a figurative journey.

9. I can challenge my reader to move into action. (Also, this is *not* a call to a sale.)

10. I can get my reader to smile or laugh at an amusing tweet.

11. I can get my reader to weep with a sad or touching tweet.

12. I can reveal secrets to my reader.

13. I can encourage my reader to never give up.

14. I can remind my reader that he is uniquely special.

15. I can remind my reader that there is something bigger, something better.

16. I can challenge or confirm my readers' assumptions.

17. I can teach my reader something in a fun way.

18. I can offer my reader a unique perspective.

19. I can remind my reader that sometimes the underdog wins.

EXERCISE 5.2

Evaluate your other social media interactions and make a list of what you do on other sites. For example, your photos on Instagram, your Tumblr images, your Pinterest stuff, your links on Facebook. All of these can be put over on Twitter. But before you post them or schedule them, ask yourself three things:

1. Are these things consistent with the brand and emotions I want portrayed to future readers?
2. Do the messages I am sending fall into one of the 21 types of content readers crave by Scott Aughtmon (or do they fit in the 19 variations in Exercise 5.1)?
3. Are these messages generous? Or, are they all about you?

EXERCISE 5.3

Return to Exercise 3.1. Using all the nouns that you collected, consider videos, images, quotes, links or articles that could be good tweets. If you connect your key words with crave-worthy content, and present it generously to your followers, you will be someone worth following! For example, if your target market is Gen Xers with a love for '80s music, you may post Janet Jackson videos, and explain how you sang into your hairbrush as a high schooler. This would put a smile on the face of any 40-something.

EXERCISE 5.4

Use Hootsuite, a web-based app, to schedule tweets from Exercise 5.3. Most of the followers in North America are active from 9AM to 5PM, Central time. Schedule 3-5 tweets a day for the next week. As your followers RT and favorite your tweets, say thank you and start conversations.

EXERCISE 5.5

Return to Exercises 3.1, 3.2 and 3.3 and review your key words. Do a Twitter search or a Google search for hashtags for your target market. Hashtags are searchable tags — you know that they are because of the # sign in the front. Your target market uses them. Hashtags are like shortcuts into conversations. If you add hashtags into your tweets, it is likely that you will be found by followers who could start conversations with you. Make a list of hashtags that apply to your target market. Make a point in every tweet you schedule to add in 2-4 hashtags. This will make you more searchable.

EXERCISE 5.6

If you are a regular blogger, don't forget to schedule your blog posts using Hootsuite. If you add the #MondayBlogs hashtag to your blog tweet, you may seen by the thousands of other bloggers around the world who do the same thing.

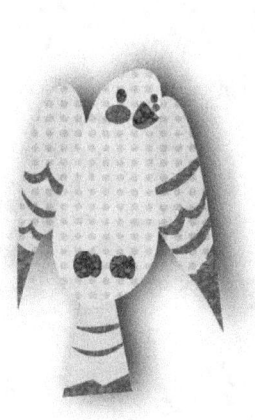

Author Confession: I do all my following on my free Twitter app on my iPhone. I find that it is the fastest and most graceful way to do searches, read bios and see lists clearly. I do it this way instead of on my laptop because speed is important to me.

Tips for tweeting about your blog post:

1. Use a URL shortener, such as bit.ly or ow.ly. The Twitter help page explains this. Hootsuite also has an option on its interface that makes this easy.

2. Tweet a good headline. Clear headlines that describe your blog post will be attractive to potential readers.

3. Don't say, "New Blog Post" in the tweet. Use the headline instead.

4. Add in hashtags from Exercise 5.5 so that your target market will see it.

5. A graphic or an image in the tweet will get more attention.

EXERCISE 5.7

Often communities on Twitter meet to talk over issues. They create a hashtag to identify themselves and may meet regularly. For example, my writers' group, 10 Minute Novelists, chats every Thursday night using the hashtag #10MinNovelists. Using your target market key words, search for chats on Google or Twitter. Then, join in and add to the conversation. Look at this as an opportunity to start relationships, not sell.

EXERCISE 5.8

More ideas for tweets:

1. What is in season. This can be the obvious, like the major holidays. But it can also be the obscure. National Pancake Day or Children's Book Day or something specific to your target market or key words.

2. What is trending. Tweet about hot topics or current events to start conversations, but only tweet about things that are consistent with your brand. If you want to be known as a light, fun, encourager to stay-at-home moms, then you may not want to discuss the latest Middle Eastern conflict, gangsta rap lyrics or the top drafting picks of the NFL.

3. What you need help with. As your followers grow, you'll have access to new opinions and advisors. Ask them for help! Ask what to make for dinner or where to buy a used car in your town. This will also start conversations.

4. What pops in your head. This is what I love about Twitter. What would be annoying on Facebook is perfectly okay here. You can tweet about the music you're listening to, the dumb thing your neighbor did, or why the weather is icky. Someone is going to identify with you and you will start a new conversation.

5. What others are celebrating. The fastest way to make friends is to listen to others and respond to their news, either good or bad.

6. What happened in your day, but don't make it too negative. Everybody can identify with a broken coffee maker, but Twitter is probably not the place to body shame your ex-boyfriend, or go into details about your childhood abuse or live tweet your loud and messy stomach virus.

7. What you messed up. Self-deprecation gets others to laugh and identify with you. I find tweeting: "I just blew it with my kids again," a great way to gain perspective.

8. What you're thankful for, both online and in real life. Take a minute and say thanks for the RT or the shout-out. Use this as a way to ask questions of others. *Hey, thanks for following me! Do you have a case of the Mondays too?*

Have Fun! **The best tweets are also spontaneous.** If we write and rewrite our tweets, we're missing the point. I think if we are unsure, feel like it has to be perfect, are overly concerned with grammar or spelling (within reason) then we're missing out on the vibrant, fast-paced environment of Twitter. Back to our stadium metaphor: if you're standing in Gillette Stadium with 70,000 NFL fans, you're not overly concerned with being perfect. You're concerned with having fun.

You know you're doing Twitter right when people are engaging with you, RT-ing you or asking you questions.

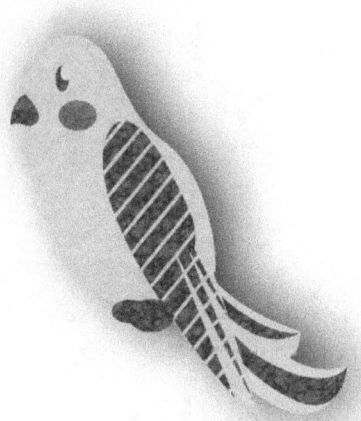

You know you're doing it right when you start to develop relationships.

You know you're doing it right when you want to spend more time on it.

You've started now. Use the suggestions in this workbook as tools, but don't become slaves to them. **If you feel like after several weeks that you aren't getting any connections, then Twitter may not be for you. You may be better suited for Instagram, Tumblr, or another social media platform. It's far better to spend your time doing what you enjoy than force something that isn't working.**

The System

By the time you get to this point in the workbook, if you have done all the exercises, you have an organized, focused set-up, a strategy that fits your brand, and ideas on how to engage your target market. Now you need to maintain this on a regular basis. It is possible to spend as little as 10 minutes a day on Twitter and maintain your following. But you must be organized and disciplined to do so.

This section explains what you need to do on a daily, weekly and monthly basis to nurture the relationships you have and find others to engage with. As you go through these tasks, understand that you will get faster. As you develop relationships, understand that you may need more time for interaction. Do what you can, when you can. Twitter is a tool for you. If you ever feel like it is too much or too overwhelming, put it away. It may not be a good fit for you.

Remember Twitter is not like Facebook; you do not have to scroll backwards through your feed to see if you missed something. As your followers grow, it will be impossible to keep up with everyone (that's why you have lists!) Do what you can and move on.

TWITTER DON'T: DO NOT ASK FOR PEOPLE TO DO STUFF FOR YOU RIGHT AWAY. YOU'VE FOLLOWED ME AT @10MINNOVELIST AND I FOLLOW YOU BACK BECAUSE YOU SEEM LIKE THE TYPE OF ARTSY PERSON I LIKE. YOU'VE COLLECTED A BUNCH OF NOUNS IN YOUR BIO AND I WANT TO ASK YOU QUESTIONS.
SO THE SECOND THAT I FOLLOW YOU BACK, **DO NOT** ASK ME TO A) DOWNLOAD YOUR FREE BOOK B) LIKE YOUR FACEBOOK PAGE C) CHECK OUT YOUR BLOG. **NO. THAT'S NOT WHAT THIS IS ABOUT.** LET ME DECIDE HOW MUCH I WANT TO BE INTERESTED IN YOU. GIVE ME A REASON. ENGAGE ME. GIVE ME CONTENT THAT I CRAVE. THEN, BECAUSE I FIND YOU FASCINATING, I'LL DO ALL THOSE THINGS. BUT THE CONNECTION BETWEEN US GOES BACK AND FORTH. I'M GETTING NOTHING OUT OF THIS EXCHANGE IF YOU BEG.

DAILY: These tasks should be done every day.

1. **Check notifications.** You'll see who followed you, who RT-ed you, who favorited you. If they are responding to something specific you said, then you've made a connection. Follow back those who would fit into your target market. Ignore those who won't, unless there's something you like about them. If you start seeing the same names and faces RT-ing and favoriting you, then they need to be on a list. They like you. You can personally thank them for the response or RT, but you don't have to. With practice, you may be able to do this in less than a minute.

2. **Check your lists.** As your followers increase, you may want to categorize them into lists. Check one of these lists daily, RT-

ing or favoriting what your new buddies have said or done. This is a great way to start conversations too! With practice, you may be able to do this in a couple of minutes.

3. Follow at least 50 people a day.

Return to Exercises 4.1-4.4 and repeat any of them to do this. Following others first is the fastest way to grow your own followers. If you read individual bios, then expect this to take longer. If you go through others' lists and follow everyone who isn't creepy or naked, then you can do this in less than five minutes with practice.

4. Mention your book, project or service only one time daily.

WEEKLY: These tasks should be done every week. Some of these can be done in less than 10 minutes, some can't.

1. Schedule your blog post. Include a good headline for Monday with the hashtag #MondayBlogs.

2. Follow the #MondayBlogs hashtag. RT as many interesting blog posts as possible. If you have time, read these blogs and leave comments. This is a great way to make friends!

3. Use #WriterWednesday or #Top10Tuesday. Find any other weekly hashtag in tweets that contain links to your blog posts.

4. Set up 2-4 tweets a day for the next week. Use Exercise 5.8 for ideas.

5. Join in any weekly chats. Follow those who participate in them. Ask questions. Make friends.

MONTHLY:

Every fourth week or so, stop following people for a few days. Then, go to an Unfollow me website (I like Tweepdash) and unfollow everyone who has not followed you back. Twitter's restrictions require a balance between your followers and those you follow. The rules are in place to curb abuse, so it's best just to clean out those followers who do not engage with you and start with new ones. Check the Twitter support page for more clarification.

OVER TIME, THE PEOPLE THAT I HAVE MET HAVE BECOME CLOSE FRIENDS. THEY ARE THE FIRST PEOPLE TO BUY MY BOOK AND HELP ME PROMOTE IT. THEY ARE MY TRIBE! THEY ARE MY RAVING FANS! IF I HADN'T BEEN WILLING TO ENGAGE WITH THEM, I WOULD HAVE NEVER HAD THIS RELATIONSHIP.

CONCLUSION

According to Twitter Live Stats, over 6,000 tweets are sent per second and over 350,000 per minute. That means that over 500 million tweets are sent per day. In 2014, over 200 billion tweets were sent. So Twitter really is nothing like yelling at a crowded football stadium. It's more like yelling in the middle of a stadium that holds a million stadiums.

The only way to be seen and heard among the gargantuan volume of tweets is to have a plan and work through it well.

Hopefully, if you have set-up your brand and bio, formulated your strategy and worked your system, you are making friends on Twitter.

I hope you look for opportunities to give and be generous to your followers and new friends. Kindness will certainly make you stick out in the crowd. As your tribe grows, you'll have loyal, enthusiastic followers who will love to buy your books, like your page, and sign up for your newsletter. You'll be thrilled with the success you have, but you'll be even happier with the friends you made.

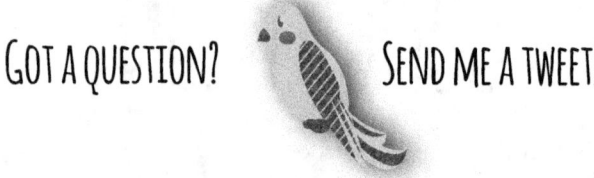

GOT A QUESTION?   SEND ME A TWEET!

@10MINNOVELIST

I'D LOVE TO HEAR HOW TWITTER WORKS FOR YOU!

ABOUT THE AUTHOR:

Katharine Grubb lives with her family in Massachusetts where she homeschools her five children, makes bread from scratch, does way too much laundry and cheers for the Patriots. She blogs at www.10minutenovelists.com. Want to chat with her? Join her every Thursday night at 9PM (Eastern Time USA) on Twitter. Follow the hashtag #10MinNovelists.

Or, join her Facebook group, 10 Minute Novelists, on Facebook for tips, encouragement and community for time-crunched writers everywhere.

OTHER BOOKS BY KATHARINE GRUBB:

FALLING FOR YOUR MADNESS:

Eccentric literature professor David approaches Laura for an unconventional, intentional, rule-filled courtship filled with poetry, flowers and bottom-less cups of tea. Laura is smitten by his humor, charm and British accent. Dating David is challenging, convicting and sometimes frustrating. There is a reason why David is bound by the laws of chivalry, both body and soul and when Laura discovers what it is, she must decide. Is David worth it? Or is he completely mad? Falling For Your Madness is a romantic comedy about ladies, gentlemen, and the power of words. **Falling For Your Madness is available in Kindle and paperback formats on Amazon.com**

Soulless Creatures:

Working-class future leader Roy Castleberry and pampered over-thinker Jonathan Campbell are 18-year-old freshmen at the University of Oklahoma who think they know everything. Roy thinks Jonathan could succeed in wooing Abby if he stopped obsessing over *Walden*. Jonathan thinks Roy could learn to be self-actualized if he'd stop flirting with every girl he meets. They make a wager: if Roy can prove that he has some poetic thought, some inner life, *A SOUL,* then Jonathan will give him the car he got for graduation. Roy takes the bet; Jonathan must be a sucker. He and Jonathan also compete for Abby, fail zoology, organize the most creative events on campus and avoid a fake ID ring led by Jonathan's brother. College life in 1986 is richer, (both experientially and financially) than either of them expected. **Soulless Creatures is available in Kindle and paperback formats on Amazon.com**

Write A Novel In 10 Minutes A Day:

Would you like to write but have no spare time? Do you not know where to begin? 'The Ten-Minute Novel' will help you sculpt a full-length piece of creative writing in just ten minutes a day. Starting with a daily practical exercise, it will help you manage your writing schedule within this time frame and help you bring your novel to life. You will be able to clarify your vision and review your time commitments, as well as understand your own abilities. Learning to observe the world around you, write quickly and tap into your unique voice will help you to create all the elements of your story and, by the time you've finished all the exercises, you'll have created something beautiful. **Write A Novel In 10 Minutes A Day is in Kindle and paperback formats on Amazon.com**

www.ingramcontent.com/pod-product-compliance
Lightning Source LLC
Chambersburg PA
CBHW062026280526
45787CB00005B/2225

* 9 7 8 1 5 1 7 6 6 7 1 1 5 *